YOUR UNIQUE PATH TO WEALTH

YOUR UNIQUE PATH TO WEALTH

CREATE A LIFE YOU LOVE OVERFLOWING
WITH ABUNDANCE, JOY, AND PURPOSE

ERIC JOHN CAMPBELL

GROUNDED GROVE
PUBLISHING

CONTENTS

PART I

PREPARE FOR YOUR JOURNEY

1

SELF-LOVE IS THE KEY TO WEALTH

AN IMPORTANT THING YOU MUST KNOW TO ATTRACT more money into your life is money is energy. The amount of money you have in your life mirrors the energy you hold within yourself. There is no point in forcing things outside of yourself to happen so that you can make more money. Your actions in your world will be the bridges for money to enter your bank account, but you must realize that your actions are just bridges.

To make the money you desire, you must first energetically become a magnet to the energy of abundance. If you're in alignment and magnetized to this energy, you'll attract all the money your heart desires once you build your bridges. Before you build bridges, you must know how to bring in and manifest the energy of abundance inside yourself. Building bridges is easy, unique to each individual, and something you can do intuitively.

Too many people have the opposite approach. They see successful people who have built thriving bridges that bring in wealth and try to build a similar bridge with no success. Don't get distracted by bridges. Just because they're something tangible the eyes can see doesn't mean they're your source of abundance. Focus instead on getting yourself to an energetic state where you become a magnet to money. The energetic state you must be in to attract all the money needed to live your heart's dream life is the frequency of self-love. When you genuinely love yourself, you have faith in your intuition as it guides you on your unique path toward a wealthy life.

The challenging part isn't loving yourself. Self-love is your natural state and is easy to embody. The hard part is letting go of everything else that gets in the way. Once you let go of all the other stuff, you'll discover that loving yourself comes as naturally as breathing. Many people will tell you to visualize your desired wealth and affirm it with positive mantras. Although this advice may come from a loving place, it may not be effective for you. If you consistently tell yourself you need more money to be happy, you may be reinforcing a pattern that makes you believe you don't deserve to feel good now.

Self-love comes on its own when you let go of everything else. You're not living in this state authentically if you must constantly use discipline to feel it. For example, there is no need to repeat empowering affirmations every morning because someone told you they would help you love yourself. If you currently have any self-love practices that you do even though you don't enjoy them, stop. You never have to do things you don't enjoy just because other people have told you they're good for you. Experiencing your natural state of self-love doesn't have to require constant effort and discipline.

Self-love comes naturally; you can't fake it and pretend to feel something you're not. When you're genuinely experiencing self-love, you bring more love into your world. Self-love is essential for building the foundation for a wealthy life that includes all the money needed to manifest your heart's desires. It doesn't matter how noble or selfless your desires are. To allow money to flow freely into your life, you must genuinely love yourself.

Many people find self-love hard to embody. If

someone feels this way, it's because they've built up stories convincing themselves they're not worthy of being loved. You're a child of the Universe, which means you were born with and carry the ability to love all you see. The infinite love of the Universe is always flowing through your heart, and you can focus this love wherever you like. Most people find it easiest to love their children or pets, but you can focus your love on celebrities, spiritual teachers, physical locations, or anything else you can imagine.

Out of all the places you can focus your love, the most important is on yourself. It's painful not to love yourself because no one can give you self-love. People can love you, but you'll have trouble feeling their love if you don't love yourself. Within each person's heart is the Universe's infinite love. The love that lives in others is the same love that lives in you.

If you have trouble loving yourself, you don't need years of therapy, self-help books, or time in nature to fix this. Loving yourself is a choice you can make right now. Like most things in your world, it's easy if you believe it's easy. All you must do to love yourself is look at your thoughts, emotions, and actions with the same unconditional love a nurturing parent has for their child. No matter what thoughts enter your mind, realize they aren't you.

Once you discover you're not your thoughts, looking at them with unconditional love is easy.

If you ever have thoughts that feel shameful or evil, love them. Without feeding your unpleasant thoughts or trying to rationalize them away, observe them with loving non-judgmental awareness. It's easy to love all your thoughts. Your ego might tell you this is a challenging thing to do, but it only believes this because of the conditioning it has received from your parents and society. Let go of old beliefs that say this is a hard thing to do, and choose to look at every thought that arises with the infinite love in your heart. Once you set the intention to love all your thoughts, you'll be surprised at how quickly doing this begins to feel natural and effortless.

In addition to your thoughts, it's essential to love your emotions. Although you can't choose your emotions, you can decide how you respond to them. For example, feeling anger is appropriate for many situations, but when you judge your anger and beat yourself up for having it, you're not loving yourself. The best way to respond to all your emotions is the same as your thoughts: love them wholeheartedly. When you feel anger, look at it with love and remind yourself you aren't the temporary anger you're experiencing.

Choose to love every emotion that arises within you. It doesn't matter if it's an emotion you like or dislike. If you experience an unpleasant emotion and then meet it with love, you'll be pleasantly surprised at how quickly that emotion passes. Feeling an intense emotion can be enjoyable if you know it's temporary. Sadness, fear, anger, and disgust can add beauty, depth, and color to your life. If you confidently know an unpleasant emotion will soon pass, it becomes easy to love.

Now that we've established that you want to love all your thoughts and emotions with the infinite love in your heart, it's time to focus on your actions. It can be tempting to judge yourself for making mistakes. You may judge yourself for doing something you wish you hadn't done or saying something you wish you could take back. By judging yourself for your previous actions, you're withholding the Universe's love and contributing to an unconscious belief that says you don't deserve money. It can be hard to see that whenever you judge yourself, you're also lowering the amount of money you receive from the Universe, but it becomes clear when you see the connection between self-love and abundance.

Everything in your world is energy, and when you align yourself with your heart, there are no limits to what you can manifest. The energy of money vibrates at the same frequency as self-love. When you genuinely love yourself, you become a powerful magnet for attracting wealth. Anytime you do something that stops you from receiving the Universe's love, you also cut yourself off from your flow of abundance.

Instead of judging yourself when you make a mistake, shower yourself with love. Use your temporary unpleasant emotions as an opportunity to see how much of the Universe's unconditional love you can focus on yourself. You always get to choose where to focus the infinite love flowing from your heart. You can focus your heart's love on all your doubts and insecurities.

You are not your thoughts, emotions, or actions; you're the observer watching those things happen. Just like a nurturing mother watches her smiling baby with unconditional love, you can choose to look at yourself with that same love. Showering your love onto everything you see or keeping it all inside doesn't change the amount of love you have in your heart. You always have an infinite well of love that can never run out.

It's important to note that loving more people doesn't earn you favor or points with the Universe.

What you're sharing isn't love if it comes with an expectation that it'll bring you something in return. However, if you share love unconditionally with no expectations, you'll feel more of it yourself since you're a channel for that love to flow through.

Recognize that you're the source of all the love you seek. You must choose to give yourself the love you crave before you can feel it from others. Learning to give yourself the love you desire is the most important lesson you need to learn to attract all the money you're looking for in your life. It's also the most essential thing you must know to live a happy life.

You can only find the love you're looking for inside your heart. This love is always available and isn't something you ever have to earn. You inherited the right to tap into the Universe's infinite love the moment you were born. The keys to the kingdom of heaven are within you. All you must do is look at all your thoughts, emotions, and actions with the love in your heart. When you do this, you create the foundation for a wealthy life while also radiating love that helps guide others back home to their heart.

2

YOUR INTUITION WILL GUIDE YOU

WITHIN EACH PERSON LIVES A SEED THAT HAS THE potential to produce endless abundance for themselves and the world. This seed in your heart contains a unique gift that only you can offer. The seed of your unique gift has the potential to dramatically change your life and the world if nurtured.

Although you may develop many talents throughout your lifetime, you have one core unique gift. From the moment of your birth, the seed of your unique gift will seek fulfillment. This seed within your heart is connected to the entire Universe and will keep attracting circumstances into your life to help it grow into its fullest expression. When you choose to nurture this seed within you, you'll experience an unshakeable feeling of joy and purpose. It's not predestined that your seed will grow into its fullest expression, but countless unseen forces are always supporting you.

If you observe nature, you'll find this pattern in many different forms of organic life. When an acorn falls off a tree, its fullest expression is to become a new tree. Not all acorns will reach their fullest expression, but the opportunity to turn into a tree is encoded within every acorn. You're also encoded with a blueprint that is ready to help you use the Universe's infinite intelligence to nurture the seed of your unique gift. The exciting thing about human potential is that the actualization of your unique gift's fullest expression is dependent on the choices that you make with your free will.

Your seed contains the blueprint for a unique gift nobody else can provide. No two seeds are alike in this world filled with billions of people. The potential for the world to flourish is unlimited. Every person alive can turn the seed of their unique gift into its fullest expression. If everyone were to do this, the world would experience billions of unique and divinely aligned gifts. By nurturing your seed into its fullest expression, you bring a beautiful new energy into the world for everyone to enjoy.

Although your world appears to be filled with an infinite number of different energies, it's all one. You're both an individual and a part of the Universe. Everyone benefits when you nurture your seed and allow it to grow into its fullest expression. The unique gift that lives within you can and will change the world if you nurture it. You'll also find no greater joy than embodying and expressing your unique gift at its fullest expression.

If you choose to nurture your seed, you'll find that the natural forces of the Universe will come together to help you express your unique gift, and your life will flow with great ease. Choosing to nurture the seed within you is the key to living a deeply satisfying life. The design of your world is always aligned with growth and abundance. By aligning yourself with the innate essence of the Universe you're a part of, your life will blossom, and you'll help the world prosper. When you align yourself with the energies of growth and abundance, you'll find the Universe supporting you in an infinite number of unseen ways because it's through you that the Universe continues to grow and experience more abundance.

The seed of your unique gift wants nothing else than to grow and will always look for the nutrients it needs to turn into its fullest expression. If you choose not to nurture the seed living within you, you'll still be able to experience moments of happiness and acquire money through intense effort. The problem with trying to force things to happen is you'll constantly be met with feelings of resistance instead of experiencing feelings of flow.

Your natural state is to grow alongside the forces of the Universe and manifest your heart's dream life. If it feels like earning money is a constant struggle, it may be because you're not nurturing your unique gift and being carried by the Universe's natural energies of growth and abundance. When you feel strong resistance, it's a sign from the Universe to change course. Resistance isn't something you have to constantly overcome; instead, it's a divine signal. When you're aligned with your unique gift, your life will flow in a way that feels natural, even when it's challenging. You'll still have times when hard work is necessary, but during those times, you'll feel an underlying energy of joy and peace.

Your intuition is the voice of your Soul and will always share with you exactly what next step to take to help turn the seed of your unique gift into its fullest expression. Every answer you seek already lives within you. Each person has the potential to express an incredible gift that has never been experienced by the world before, but they also can choose not to share their unique gift.

You may be choosing not to nurture your unique gift because of the discomfort that arises from listening to and following your intuition. It may seem easier and less painful to silence your intuition and listen to the voices of others outside of yourself instead. If you haven't been listening to your intuition for a long time, you may believe you don't have a wise inner voice.

Everyone has a wise inner voice, and following yours is the key to nurturing the seed of your unique gift into its fullest expression. Your intuition always knows what next step to take in your life. Learning how to listen to and follow your intuition is the most important thing you can ever do for your happiness and the collective. If you lose your connection to your intuition and instead prioritize other voices outside yourself, you'll end up lost and unable to nurture your unique gift.

Your intuition is part of your uniqueness; only you know what it sounds like and how to follow it. Your intuition is often called your inner voice, following your heart, or the voice of your Soul. It doesn't matter what you call your intuition or how it communicates with you; what matters is that you listen to and follow it.

When you first start following your intuition, you'll likely be guided to take actions that make no sense to your ego, even though they're necessary to help nurture your unique gift. The mind you were born with is a beautiful creative tool necessary for living on Earth as a human being. Your mind has created your present life circumstances and, in this very moment, is creating your future. What you want to avoid is confusing this magnificent creative tool with your Soul. Your mind is such a powerful tool that it has created an identity for yourself that is built upon many different ideas about who you are, what makes you this way, and where your life is headed.

We'll use the word *ego* to refer to the sum of all your mind's ideas of who it thinks you are. Your ego isn't built on anything substantial and instead is made out of thoughts that are as intangible as clouds. You are not your ego, and you are not your thoughts. Your true self is your eternal Soul, and you've chosen to incarnate here on Earth to have a temporary human experience. Your ego will disappear when your human body dies, but your Soul exists outside of time.

The ego your mind created is necessary for you to function in daily life. While living inside a human body, you need a story about who you are and what is shaping you, but you must remember who you are underneath this story. The goal isn't to transcend or get rid of your ego. What you're seeking is a partnership between your Soul and ego. When you know deep down that you're a Soul that is living temporarily as an ego and human body, you'll have the courage to listen to and follow your intuition.

You must trust your intuition above all other voices to see your world clearly. If you believe other people's words are more important than your intuition, you'll see their version of the world. The lens through which your Soul sees the world is rooted in growth and abundance, mixed with the qualities of your unique gift. Most of the voices you hear in the collective at this time come from the speaker's ego instead of their Soul. If you allow the voice of another person's ego to be the source of your truth, you'll see a world filled with fear and scarcity.

On the other hand, you may have found some voices outside yourself who speak words of love, which you can tell originate from the speaker's Soul.

If this is your experience, you still want to prioritize your intuition above their words. If you rely on the voice of another, no matter how pure their intentions are, eventually, they'll say something that isn't aligned with your truth. When this happens, you'll either suffocate what is true for you or lose the sense of foundation and security you found in that person.

When it comes to your life, your intuition is the wisest voice you'll ever hear. You may enjoy and learn from the wisdom of others, but they can't be your north star. You must find your center in your Soul, which means your attachment to the outer world is never more powerful than your commitment to your intuition. Living this way will give you inner peace and clarity, regardless of what is happening outside yourself.

You must look beyond what the people near you are doing and learn to follow your intuition. All the answers you seek are already within you, on a level deeper than your mind. Your intuition knows the exact blueprint for turning your unique seed into its fullest expression and will guide you step-by-step. Books, videos, and podcasts can help mirror what your intuition is trying to communicate to you, but they can't be the source of your truth.

Within you now lives an endless well of potential ideas that have never been brought into your world. Your intuition is the well from which all creative visions are drawn. You can never fully understand your intuition intellectually, but you can feel it. When you listen to and follow your intuition, there is a sense of being guided by a divine force that exists to make your life better. This inner presence you feel is the Universe desiring to express more growth and abundance through you. The seed of your unique gift is always trying to realize its fullest expression. This seed of yours knows what nutrients it needs to thrive and is trying to communicate with you now; *can you hear what it's saying?*

Each person connects with their intuition in a way that is specific to them. By going within, you'll find the unique way that your Soul wants to communicate with you. The key to hearing this quiet voice within is to find ways to lower the outer stimulation of your environment and your mind. Once your environment and mind are quiet, it'll be easy to hear your intuition.

Your Soul is always trying to communicate with you, even if you've been avoiding your intuition for many years. At first, it'll be hard to discern the difference between your intuition and the voices you've inherited from others that echo inside your mind, but with practice, it'll become easy. It helps to be alone in nature, but it's not necessary. Even in an apartment in the middle of a busy city, you can put on headphones, play relaxing music, and go within.

After you've created a relaxing environment and are seated in a comfortable position, focus all your attention on your heart while taking slow, deep breaths. Initially, your mind will be loud and cycle through many seemingly random thoughts. While this happens, keep as much of your energy as possible centered on your heart and observe the thoughts that arise without judgment.

While doing this practice, you'll likely observe some thoughts that trigger you, and you'll feel those thoughts begin to pull your energy away from your center. Whenever your thoughts begin to pull your energetic center away from your heart or if you find yourself temporarily lost in them, become aware that you've drifted, and then return your energy back to your heart.

Always remember, you are not your thoughts. Although you'll likely feel tempted to fight the thoughts you don't like, you must continually bring your energetic center back to your heart. Each time you get caught up in the stories of your thoughts or try to fight them, you temporarily lose your sense of awareness and drift away from your intuition. Instead of judging yourself when this happens, practice patience while acknowledging this is an essential part of the process.

An easy thing you can do to help you stay energetically centered on your heart while doing this exercise is to place your hands on top of it. By touching your heart with your hands, you help anchor your energetic center there. You can also visualize breathing the energy of clarity into your body with each inhale and imagining all the stagnant energy leaving your body with each exhale.

There is no right or wrong way to connect with your intuition. Any time you spend learning how to connect with your intuition is priceless, no matter what the outcome is. Although the exercise I mentioned may be helpful, it's one of an infinite number of ways you can connect with your intuition. The only important thing is that you take time to find inner stillness while creating the intention to listen to the voice of your Soul.

Each time you connect with your intuition, you'll know you're speaking directly with your Soul because your body will feel a profound sense of peace. Soon, you'll look forward to connecting with your intuition because every time you do, it'll make your body feel amazing. Your Soul and the Universe want you to know how deeply they love you and how proud of you they are. Although it's nice to hear these words through this book, it's more nourishing when you hear and feel them inside your heart.

PART II

WALK YOUR PATH

3

MONEY IS LIKE A CAT

A BIG OBSTACLE MANY PEOPLE FACE WHEN TRYING TO attract more money is wanting it desperately. The desire for money is beautiful, but if your craving for it is so intense that you can't enjoy your life until it arrives, you're blocking your flow of abundance. If you spend most of your energy trying to figure out how to manifest more money into your life, you're doing more harm than good. The energy of money is gentle and wants to nourish you, but when you start craving it obsessively, it'll get scared and run away from you.

It's helpful to think of the energy of money as a cat. If you try too hard to get a cat's affection, it'll sense your neediness and run away. On the other hand, if you stay focused on loving yourself, the cat will eventually come to you and give you its affection. The energy of obsession repels the energy of money. If you believe you must have more money before you can experience inner peace and happiness, you'll never stop chasing it, and whatever you chase will run away from you.

You can also think of money as a beautiful spiritual teacher. The energy of money is teaching you how to love yourself. If spending most of your time obsessing over money brought more of it into your life, you would never stop thinking about it. Instead of believing that more money will bring you a life you love, realize that every feeling you wish to experience already lives within you. By finding the feelings you wish to experience within first, you'll discover that all the money you need to live your heart's dream life comes on its own.

If the money your heart desires still hasn't entered your life yet, it's because you're still mastering self-love. You're in the process of returning to your most natural state of trusting your intuition and living a joyful life where you don't have to constantly worry about where more money will come from next. If all you did after reading this book was spend half as much energy on thinking about money as you do now, you would likely attract more of it. Most people think about money too much.

When you focus too much of your energy on where more money will come from next, you'll notice feelings of uneasiness and tightness in your body. Ironically, if you believe more money will give you inner peace, you'll seek it desperately and experience less peace. Let go of focusing on how you can make more money and instead learn to live happily now. After giving up your aggressive hunt for more money, you'll notice your life already contains infinite beauty. When you switch your focus onto loving yourself, you'll find that the money you desire will come in its own rhythm and timing.

If you focus on finding peace and happiness first, sooner or later, the cat will come to you with its affection. The energy of money can't wait to unite with you and desires nothing more than to nurture your unique gift, but out of love, it won't come until you let go of your desperate need to have it. Let go of the heavy expectation that more money will give you the feelings you wish to experience. Once you realize you don't need more money to feel good, you'll attract more of it into your life because your outer world mirrors what is occurring within you.

You must have faith in what your heart knows to

be true, or you'll get lost in the illusion of outer appearances. The most dominant belief in your society now says that discipline and hustling are the only ways to manifest more money into your life. Switching your focus onto loving yourself takes courage.

You must continually choose to focus on something that seems to go against what the majority of your society believes. Rather than focus on how you'll make more money, give that area of your life less attention. Let go of the idea that you'll feel better when you have more money and instead focus on how great you're feeling now. Living a life filled with self-love is easy; this way of living is your natural state and is how you're born to live.

At its core, self-love is trusting what you know to be true for you, even when the people giving you advice love you very much and only want what is best for you. You were born with a heart's dream life that only you know. Your heart's dream life might be as grand as creating a world-changing company or as simple as living in a small cabin in the woods. If you explain your heart's dream life to a loved one, they can't feel it intuitively like you can, so you must prioritize what you know to be true within yourself.

Trusting your intuition is how you'll create a life you love instead of defaulting to the life your parents and society have conditioned you to believe you want. Having confidence and faith in your intuition isn't reckless or egotistical; it's an expression of self-love.

4

NURTURE YOUR HEART'S DESIRES

YOUR EGO WILL CREATE MANY DESIRES THAT MAKE YOU feel you must fulfill them to be happy. If you have a desire and are unsure whether it comes from your ego or your heart, notice how it feels. Your ego's desires always carry the underlying energy of fear. If you're pursuing one of your ego's desires, you'll feel you're not okay now and won't be at peace until your desire is met. Another quality of your ego's desires is scarcity. If your desire contains the energy of scarcity, you'll believe that you must act fast and force things to happen; otherwise, you'll miss out on a significant opportunity.

Your heart's desires feel different. If a desire comes from your heart, there will be a feeling of peace, as if the fulfillment of your desire is inevitable and will manifest in divine timing that is outside of your control. When you nurture the seed of your unique gift and move closer to its fullest expression, you'll notice new desires arise in your heart. Pursuing your heart's desires helps nurture and grow the seed of your unique gift.

Your heart's desires always feel joyful from the moment they appear until they're fulfilled. On the other hand, your ego's desires always bring uncomfortable feelings of tension the entire time you're moving toward their fulfillment. If you fulfill one of your ego's desires, you'll feel great for a short moment until a new one arises, bringing back feelings of tension. This hamster wheel of constantly pursuing desires that lead to endless tension is why many people try to give up desiring things completely. If you've spent your whole life chasing your ego's desires, you may believe that all desires create suffering.

Pursuing your heart's desires is one of the most fun parts of being alive. When you begin enjoying the feeling of sitting with your heart's desires, with faith that their fulfillment is inevitable, you can enjoy the present moment while also being excited about what will soon enter your life. The key is to become aware of the difference between desires that come from your ego and your heart. Once you know the difference, you can surrender your ego's desires and focus all your newfound energy on enjoying the present moment.

When you're excited about your heart's desires, that excitement is felt in the present. There is no waiting for a future moment to be happy when you're aligned with your heart's desires. Often, you'll only know what the fulfillment of your heart's desires feels like while having little to no idea of what they'll look like. Trust your heart's feeling when you sense something wonderful is on its way to you. Your intuition is leading you to a life that is more joyful and magical than your ego can envision.

Your mind is a wonderful creative tool. When it's time to use this tool to manifest your heart's desires, you'll receive guidance from your intuition. You never have to force the use of manifesting techniques to realize your heart's desires; if you feel like you do, you're probably pursuing one of your ego's desires. Everything about your heart's desires will feel light and easy. If thinking about your current desires makes you feel heavy and tired, ask your intuition where your desires are coming from.

The Universe is always seeking more growth and abundance through you and doesn't want you to feel tension in the pursuit of your heart's desires. Manifesting your unique version of heaven on earth is designed to be an exciting adventure. Trust your intuition when it whispers your heart's desires to you and tells you how to fulfill them. At first, your intuition will help bring awareness to all the desires you currently carry that come from your ego.

Once you surrender your ego's desires, you'll experience complete presence in the only moment that exists: the present. Everything unfolding around you now is breathtakingly beautiful, but you can't see it if your vision is clouded by your ego's desires. When you surrender all the desires that come from your ego, you'll no longer wait for your future to be happy; instead, you'll find an incredibly beautiful life in the moment you're already in.

Your unique gift can only reach its fullest expression when your energy is anchored in the present. If you split your energy between the past and present or present and future, you'll be unable to commit your vital life force energy to your unique gift. You're already where your heart longs to be, which is the present moment. You may move to a new city or country further down the line as you keep listening to and following your intuition, but what your heart desires more than anything is for you to be fully present wherever you are in the world.

You'll notice something peculiar happens when you keep following your intuition. The more you listen to that still voice within, the more present you become. Through your own experience, you'll discover that your ego can only exist in a perceived past or future, and your intuition can only be heard in the present. While learning how to connect with your intuition, you'll notice that meditating or practicing any other activity that brings you more fully into the present makes your intuition much easier to hear.

Every step you take toward the fulfillment of your heart's desires will bring you more fully into the present. It's only in the present that the veils your ego has placed out of fear that mask the beauty of the world are removed. The present is where true life exists. When you see the world clearly, you're left with speechless beauty. Your Soul has been trying to help you return to the beauty of the present all along. When you're fully present, all illusions are released, and the seed of your unique gift effortlessly finds its fullest expression.

5

YOU'RE BORN TO BE ABUNDANT

THE ENERGY OF MONEY IS A MANIFESTATION OF THE Universe's infinite love for you and is available to anyone who seeks it. When you have a strong desire in your heart to become wealthy, it's because you have a longing to more fully express your unique gift to the world, which requires you to have more money. When you realize that your heart's desire for wealth exists because you want to have more financial freedom to share your unique gift with others, you'll no longer feel any guilt when attempting to manifest it.

It's impossible to fully share your unique gift when your financial situation forces you to participate in a job you dislike or worry about what you'll eat and where you'll sleep. There is a widespread belief in your world that desiring money is bad and that wealthy people aren't happy. This belief only has its power if you look outside yourself for answers instead of looking toward your personal experience.

Ask your heart: *would my life be better if I had more money?* If the answer is yes, that is a beautiful answer and isn't something you must deny or feel shame over. A balanced and healthy love for money is a form of self-love. You desire more money because it's an energy that allows you to take care of your mental, physical, and spiritual health. If you deny your heart's desire for more wealth, you'll end up in a painful internal conflict when you work to manifest it.

There is nothing dark or evil about wanting to be wealthy. The energy of money is beautiful and wants to nurture you. Desiring more money is only a problem when someone prioritizes the pursuit of it above everything else. If someone's main goal in life is to become rich, they'll blind themselves to the love inside their heart. A healthy love for money comes the moment you realize it's only a tool.

The Universe is one living being that is always conspiring in your favor. Once you realize that the energy of money can help you more fully express your unique gift to the world, you'll see that everyone benefits when you become wealthy. The Universe wants you to live in a beautiful area where you feel safe and eat healthy, nutritious food so you have the energy to share your unique gift.

You're the only person in the world who can express the Universe's love in the specific way you're able to. We're all one, which means your happiness and abundance benefit everyone. Becoming a wealthy individual makes you a beacon of light with the creative capacity to love the world in a unique way that no one else can replicate.

You are love, and within you now lies the seed of a unique gift that will change the world in a beautiful way when fully nurtured by the energy of money. Everyone you've ever met, including anyone jealous or hateful towards wealthy individuals, benefits when you manifest the money needed to fulfill your heart's desires.

You may be doubting these words if you're not clear on what your unique gift is. If you don't know what your unique gift is yet, it doesn't mean you don't have one. You manifested these words into your life because the Universe is preparing you to change the world in a loving way that only you can do. Instead of viewing the desire for money as a selfish wish, realize it's the best way to love your world.

Self-love means loving the world because you're a child of the Universe, and it's through you that you can love everybody else. If you restrict your flow of abundance because you don't believe you're worthy enough to receive it, you won't get all your needs met and will be forced to withhold your heart's flow of love from the world. You're born to be wealthy. The Universe has blessed you with great luck, and everybody you attract has come to help you grow into the wealthy, fully-expressed individual you're born to be.

Your entire life has been preparing you to share the love you have in your heart with the world, and the most important step you can take now is to fully open yourself up to receive all the abundance the Universe wants to give you. It's time for you to become wealthy far more effortlessly than your ego believes is possible so you can nurture your unique gift, which is currently a seed in your heart waiting patiently to bloom.

6

MONEY IS FUEL

Money has no preferences as to how you use it. The energy of money is fuel that you can use toward anything you desire. Just like a car uses fuel to operate, you can use money to fuel your creative expression. Money is the substance that gives you the freedom to create in your world. Although it's possible and enjoyable to express your creativity without much money, it's often easier with more money.

You unlock incredible magic when you have the freedom to redirect your energy away from the need to survive and purely toward your creative expression. You can become a well of limitless creativity when the need to make more money is no longer a heavy, energetic weight holding you back. You'll experience tremendous freedom in your creative expression when you're no longer forced to do things you dislike to survive.

You were born into this world to feel safe and free to play. When your struggle to earn money goes away, your inner child will feel free to create beautiful new things for no other reason than it feels wonderful to your body, mind, and Soul. Take a moment to visualize your wealthy future self, fully expressing the creative impulses of your inner child. *How does it feel to play and create for the simple joy of expressing what wants to be birthed through your heart?*

Your ego is likely creating resistance now because you haven't received an answer yet as to how more money will come, but you must see that the *how* already lives within you. The specifics of how you'll generate wealth are unique to your life and can only come from within. The beautiful truth is that everyone who has a genuine, heartfelt desire to become wealthy can realize their dream.

If your heart wants to become wealthy, it means your Soul already has a clear and precise path for how you can make it happen. Before you're able to receive this inner plan, you must clear and purify all the old beliefs that are getting in the way of your ability to manifest more abundance. Although you may feel that you don't have limiting beliefs about money or that the ones you do have aren't stopping you now, it's important to acknowledge that these beliefs are often unconsciously learned from your parents and society.

Many people in your world have inherited beliefs that say making money is hard or evil. Often, people are limited by beliefs about money that they don't know they carry. If you're afraid of becoming wealthy in a way that is aligned with your heart, ask yourself if there are any hidden beliefs creating a glass ceiling over your ability to manifest more money.

There is so much beauty in being a wealthy individual who shares what is on their heart freely, without restriction. Realize that the hate many people appear to have toward those who are wealthy comes from a misunderstanding that wealth is limited. There is an infinite amount of wealth in the world that is constantly increasing. The world's abundance will never stop growing, thanks to the endless inspiration and resourcefulness that lie within the human spirit.

Although many people believe that other people's wealth takes away from their own, this isn't true when someone makes their money in a heartfelt way. Every time someone becomes wealthier by following their intuition, they increase the abundance of the human collective. A great example of this is the human spirit that generated the solution of sustainable energy in a world that used to fear it was running out of the only thing they believed could run society—fossil fuels. No matter what challenges humans face as a collective, they will always be able to solve them if they believe in their ability to do so.

The same concept applies to the generation of wealth. There will always be opportunities to create more wealth in ways that haven't been discovered yet. I share this with you now to help you see that when you become wealthy and have more creative fuel to share your unique gift, the world benefits. Everyone wins whenever someone manifests more wealth in a heartfelt way, and it's through this discovery that you won't take it personally when others feel jealous or threatened by your financial abundance.

You're a beautiful and kind-hearted Soul who deserves to have all the fuel you need to express the infinite well of love living within your heart. When you share your unique gift and become abundant as a result, you'll manifest a life so beautiful that it'll show others what they're capable of and inspire them to create a life they love.

7

YOU'RE THE DIRECTOR OF
YOUR LIFE

AN ESSENTIAL PART OF BECOMING WEALTHY IS realizing that money is only one manifestation of true abundance. Before you can see the money you're seeking appear in physical form, you must first plant the seeds of abundance within yourself. All manifestations in the outer world start as a seed within someone's consciousness. You can think of your consciousness as an inner garden that must be nurtured.

The way you cultivate your inner garden is by making sure you plant beliefs that match the life your heart wants to live while removing any limiting beliefs that are like weeds preventing your garden from growing. *Do you know that wealth is both limitless and easy to manifest when you follow your heart? Do you believe you're one with the Universe and the dreams living within your heart exist because you're born to manifest them?* These are examples of abundant beliefs you want to plant and nurture inside your inner garden.

Your ego likely has lots of doubts and wants to know the specifics of how you'll make more money, but it can't yet see that you could be given the precise plan on how your unique gift can make all the money your heart desires and it wouldn't work if you have a limiting belief in your inner garden, such as "you can't make a living doing what you love." The things you manifest in the outer material world are a mirrored reflection of the beliefs you plant and nurture internally.

Although the world holds a popular belief that life is unfair and each person is a victim of forces outside of their control, you don't have to hold this belief in your consciousness. You aren't the one creating anybody else's life, but when it comes to your life, you're the one and only director. If you don't like your life, you have the power to change it. You're the author of your life story, and although you can't change another person's story, you can choose who you allow into your life and how you let them treat you. Taking responsibility for your life is how you free yourself from the feeling of powerlessness. Ask yourself: *am I a victim, or am I the creator of my life?*

If you look outside yourself for people to tell you how the world works, you'll manifest people giving you evidence that feeds the beliefs you've already grown within yourself. Stop looking outside yourself for answers or validation and go within. Instead of looking to the lives of others for evidence of how your world works, look at your life experience and draw your own conclusions.

Everyone alive on your planet now has chosen to incarnate on Earth with a very specific mission. The journey of each Soul is unique to that individual, and the lessons you're here to learn in this lifetime are different from the lessons other Souls are here to learn. One Soul may have chosen to incarnate here on Earth in this lifetime to experience life with lots of money, while another may have come here to learn how to give up all material possessions and live as a hermit in the woods.

Only you know why your Soul has decided to incarnate here on Earth, which is why you're the only one who should be telling yourself what the important people, things, and experiences to value in your life are. Profound wisdom for one person could be detrimental advice to another. There are no universal truths that you should blindly follow just because your parents and society say or imply that you should.

Go within and ask your heart: *why am I here on Earth, and what is it that my Soul desires to experience in this lifetime?* The answer to this question will help you receive all the wealth needed to live your heart's dream life. Every desire in your heart has been given to you by your Soul for an essential reason. Instead of feeling shame around your heart's desires or believing they're unrealistic, look at them as your north star.

Once you wake up to the creative power you hold, you'll immediately begin using your power to manifest your heart's desires. Nothing will come remotely close to making you as happy and fulfilled as pursuing the desires in your heart. The family you were born into and the society you grew up in had certain preconceived ideas about what provides people with happiness, but their ideas may not reflect what makes your heart happy.

The point isn't to go against your parents and society by doing the opposite of what you've been raised to believe will make you happy. The point is that you have to go within and ask your heart what life you want to create for yourself while you're alive for this relatively short period of time on Earth. There are no rules as to what you can or can't manifest. You're living in an unprecedented time in human history, with creative opportunities that weren't possible only one generation ago. Instead of limiting yourself to the lives people have created in the past, give yourself complete creative freedom to burn all old templates and start anew.

You're a limitless, eternal Soul of pure light having a temporary human experience. While you're alive on Earth, express the fullness of everything that wants to be birthed through your heart. Money has an essential role to play in this dance because it's the fuel needed to fulfill the vision of the life you want to create for yourself, which you can feel deep within your heart. Your Soul chose to come to this world with immense enthusiasm because it knew you would wake up to your creative power and build your unique version of heaven on earth that is infinitely more beautiful and magical than your ego can imagine.

8

DO WHAT YOU LOVE NOW

THE ENERGY OF MONEY IS MAGNETIC TO JOY. IF YOU want to manifest the wealth needed to live your heart's dream life, you must find work you love. An easy way to discover this work is to ask yourself: *what would I do if I had unlimited money?* The thing you feel like you need more money to do is pointing you toward the unique gift you're here on Earth to share. If you're ready to become wealthy, you must go within and discover what work your heart feels inspired to do.

Work will take up a large percentage of your life, which is why it's so important to find something you love doing. If your only priority in finding work is to make as much money as possible, you'll create a life your heart doesn't enjoy. You'll attract abundance in all areas of your life when you find work that you feel inspired to do purely for the joy of doing it. Money is a by-product of finding and participating in activities that ignite the fiery passion of your Soul.

If you don't like the work you're doing now, find out how to make the transition toward doing work you love. If what you're passionate about can't immediately pay your bills, find ways to do it in your free time. Every minute you spend working on the thing you love begins building momentum for a brand-new career. You can do work you love while keeping a job you dislike to pay your bills, but what you must never do is completely give up the thing that lights up your Soul. Every time you do work your heart deeply enjoys, you'll feel passionate energy fill your body that can't come from any other source.

You were born to express the Universe's infinite love in a unique form that nobody else can replicate. It's up to you whether or not you want to share your unique gift with the world. If you love to paint, paint. If you love to write, write. If you love to dance, dance. All that matters is that you do the thing you want to do now instead of waiting for more money to come before you start doing it. Many people have dreams of what they want to do in the future, telling themselves they can't afford to do it now without acknowledging that the only thing actually stopping them is fear.

You're fully capable of doing a version of what you love to do right now, regardless of how much money you have in your bank account. If you want to direct music videos, start by creating passion projects over the weekend with your friends. If you'd like to open a bakery, start by baking special cupcakes for your family once a week. When you commit yourself to doing what you love now, ways to manifest more money will soon appear. These new bridges to wealth will likely manifest as inspired ideas that suddenly drop into your mind while you're focusing on your passion.

You don't need to struggle now with the hope that one day, you'll get lucky and finally be able to live a life you love. Instead of waiting to be happy in your future, find ways to prioritize and incorporate what makes you happy into your present life. There is no future outside this present moment you're experiencing. Instead of waiting for a future to arrive where you get to do what you love, begin integrating your dream life into your present life until they merge into one. Ask yourself: *what would my life look like if I were wealthy, and how can I start to live that way now?*

There are likely some creative ideas you have now that you'd like to pursue but can't because you don't have the necessary financial resources. Instead of focusing on what you can't do, focus on what you can do. The journey to your unique version of heaven on earth starts with taking one step forward in a new direction. If you want to create an abundant life your heart loves, ask yourself: *what simple action can I take right now to start building momentum?*

The world you're living in is flexible and adapts to the energies you cultivate within yourself. The most important thing you can do now is take one step in the direction your heart wants to go. The first step is the most important one and is what your wealthy future self will be most grateful for. You can't wait for more money to enter your life before you start living the life your heart dreams of. You must first generate energetic momentum by doing the thing you love before the Universe can help you manifest more money through new opportunities, ideas, and synchronicities.

Once you start doing what you love, you'll find yourself receiving divinely inspired ideas that gently guide you down a beautiful and abundant path.

While walking this path, money will come to you so effortlessly that you'll forget why you ever felt there was a scarcity of it in the world. All the money your heart desires comes when you focus on the joy of working instead of waiting for more money to make you happy and solve all your problems.

Whatever your ego believes it needs to be happy is an illusion. Nothing outside yourself can deliver happiness in a way that can't be received from within. What your heart wants is to feel a certain way that your ego believes can only be felt through manifesting certain people, things, or experiences into your life. The truth is, you can choose to feel and live the life your ego believes you need more money to experience now.

Instead of waiting for more money to give you permission to express your creativity, start now. If you begin living the life you think you need more money to live, you'll find the money comes on its own when you're preoccupied with the simple joy of expressing your creativity. Many people believe that when they have more money, they'll have the energy to do the things they love, but the opposite is true. You must begin doing what you enjoy before you'll feel more energy and inspiration.

Taking ten minutes out of your day to express

your greatest passion in some form will give you energy that lasts an entire week. If you're not expressing the love and creative life force within your heart, you'll feel constantly tired, regardless of how much time you spend working a job you dislike to pay the bills. Don't use your present job as an excuse for why you can't start living the life you believe you must be wealthy to live. The essence of what you believe you'll be able to do once you have more money can be felt and experienced now.

If your ego is putting up resistance and coming up with a long list of reasons why it's not possible to start doing any form of what you love now, ask yourself if there are any creative alternatives you haven't thought of. For example, if you want more money so you can travel, you can find somewhere within an hour's walk or drive from where you live and act as if you've flown across the world to be there. You could also spend a weekend morning people-watching at a café you've never been to.

Your creative options for living a life you love are limitless, but before you can open up these possibilities, you must surrender the belief that you're a victim of your present financial circumstances and that you'll only be happy once you're wealthy. If you have enough money to meet your essential needs but still feel that you don't enjoy your life, there is likely an underlying reason that goes deeper than a lack of money. If you're scared to pursue the thing your heart really wants to do, you can find peace of mind by admitting that to yourself instead of hiding behind the belief that you must be rich before you can do what you love.

You're completely capable and deserving of attracting more money into your life, but you'll be unable to if you're using the pursuit of wealth as an excuse for avoiding the true fear you're running from. If you've been putting off all possible forms of doing the thing your heart most deeply wants to do, ask yourself why. The answer to this question is how you unlock all the abundance you've been waiting to receive from the Universe.

9

LET GO OF UNHEALTHY RELATIONSHIPS

A COMMON FEAR THAT CAN STOP PEOPLE FROM manifesting an abundant life is the fear of other people's envy. Many people believe that a lack of money is the root cause of their suffering. When you become wealthy, your presence alone will likely trigger some people who believe that having more money would solve all their problems. When others are envious of your abundance, they may unconsciously distance themselves from you or project their negative judgments toward rich people onto you.

It's not your fault if some of the people you used to be close with begin to distance themselves when you attract more abundance into your life. Part of becoming a wealthy individual includes outgrowing relationships that no longer serve you. If you have to let go of some unhealthy relationships in your life when you manifest more abundance, know that it's to create space for beautiful new relationships to bloom.

It's your responsibility to create a life you love, but you can't control how other people respond to the life you manifest. Becoming more abundant will likely bring a significant change to your relationships, but this change is positive and will bring immense joy into your life. Every relationship in your life is your choice, and if you feel in your heart that you must distance yourself from certain people, trust your intuition.

One of the most influential relationships in your life is with the family you were born into. Many people had a beautiful relationship with their family growing up and continue to look to them as a source of great love, comfort, and joy. However, there are also some people who didn't have healthy relationships with their family growing up and have learned that the best thing they can do for their well-being is to distance themselves.

Unlike the message society often portrays through movies, news, and books, not everyone's highest potential is to look to the family they were born into for a sense of home and comfort. Some people may have felt like the black sheep in their family and always longed for more heartfelt connections than the ones they experienced growing up. Other people may need to temporarily distance themselves from their families to go on a journey of self-discovery. Each person's family dynamics are different, but you must realize that no matter what the relationship dynamic is, you always have a choice. The level of emotional involvement you choose to have with anyone in your life is up to you.

Go towards the people who make you feel safe and loved, whoever they may be. You'll feel empowered when every relationship you're in is a choice rather than something you feel forced into. The people who truly love you will always support you, no matter where your heart leads you. If any of the people in your life are triggered by your abundance but are doing their best to work through it, those people are coming from a place of deep love and respect.

However, if any of the people in your life act mean when you become more abundant, and you don't feel an underlying current of love from them, it may be time to re-evaluate that relationship. There is never a need to stay in an unhealthy relationship. If your logic, intuition, and dreams repeatedly tell you to cut energetic cords with a specific person or group of people, there is a significant reason why.

When you manifest more wealth, you may find it hard to stay intimately connected with some of the people you've spent time with in the past. It's okay to stop spending time with someone you used to be close with if you know deep in your heart that the relationship is no longer healthy for you. On the other hand, you may already be in close relationships with beautiful Souls who will grow with you as you attract greater abundance into your life. Appearances don't matter; what is important are the intuitive feelings within your heart.

The relationships you choose to nurture dramatically affect the life you build for yourself. You can't create a life of freedom and genuine joy if you're holding on to people who continuously pull you into unhealthy lifestyle choices and feelings of unworthiness. There is a balance to be had here. You don't want to immediately cut out everyone in your life with the belief that all your current relationships are unhealthy.

Every relationship in your life serves a greater purpose. While you're here on Earth, your Soul is always learning. If you weren't faced with any challenging relationships, you wouldn't grow in the way your Soul desires to. But just because someone's challenging energy has helped you grow in the past doesn't mean it's necessary to keep them in your life. You must honor and trust the guidance coming from within and prioritize it over appearances.

Your heart already knows who is a beautiful light in your life and who you need to distance yourself from. Letting go of relationships that no longer serve you is an act of self-love. Once you distance yourself from people who aren't healthy for you, you can love them from afar and thank them for teaching your Soul valuable lessons.

The world is filled with countless wonderful people who want to see you thrive in all areas of your life. No matter where your heart takes you, know that you're loved infinitely more deeply than your ego can imagine. If you must remove yourself from an unhealthy relationship, know that there are many people eagerly waiting to love and nourish you in the way your heart craves. You deserve to be truly loved as you are now, for no other reason than you are a one-of-a-kind expression of the Universe's infinite love.

10

FEEL GROUNDED WHILE ALIVE ON EARTH

THERE IS AN INFINITE AMOUNT OF ABUNDANCE available in your world. Even though the Universe has countless blessings it wants to share, you may have noticed that sometimes spiritual people struggle financially. At some point, you've likely asked yourself why many loving, spiritual people struggle to attract money. There is a paradox here because the people who tend to have the most expansive internal beliefs about what is possible are many times the most financially limited.

The reason some spiritual people may struggle to become wealthy is that they have trouble grounding their energy on Earth. To manifest in the physical world you exist in now, you must primarily root your energy here and not away in other planes of consciousness. The more grounded you are in this world, the more easily you'll be able to manifest material wealth. Learning how to ground your energy is an important part of creating a wealthy life.

Having the ability to access spiritual realms is a wonderful gift that can give your life vision and purpose, but once you receive downloads from the Universe, you must root that energy down here on Earth. It's not enough to be inspired and then wait for your manifestations to come to you without taking action. There is a time for relaxing and waiting for things to grow, but there is also a time to act on divine inspiration.

Many people who struggle to feel grounded on Earth believe that manifesting abundance is about setting the intention and then waiting for their vision to come true by some force outside of their control. People with this belief may buy lottery tickets, believing their intentions will help them win millions of dollars. Winning the lottery may be the destiny for an extremely limited number of people, but most likely, you'll need to take greater amounts of action to become wealthy. To manifest an abundant life, you must act on the instructions you receive from your heart. If you receive divine guidance from journaling or meditation and then don't act on it, the Universe can't help you manifest the money your heart desires.

Part of becoming grounded may include taking actions that other spiritual people disapprove of. Instead of following the guidance of other spiritual teachers, go within and ask your heart. Your unique Soul path in this lifetime is different from everybody else's. There can be great beauty in enjoying the material and carnal pleasures of your world. Things like eating meat, having sex, drinking alcohol, and going to the gym don't make you a non-spiritual person.

If you want to manifest an abundant life, you must take actions that your wealthy future self would do. Go into meditation and visualize a day in the life of your wealthy future self. *What does your daily routine look like? How do you feel while participating in your daily activities?* The more you can bring the daily habits of your wealthy future self into your present life, the quicker you'll be able to manifest the abundance you desire.

You can become a wealthy healer and artist if that is what your heart desires. There are no rules in your world that say certain groups of people can't become abundant based on their profession. Thanks to modern-day technology, there are far more wealthy healers and artists now than there have ever been before, and this number will only grow as time goes on.

Abundance comes to those who find a balance between their higher and lower chakras. By practicing yoga, meditating, working with crystals, reading tarot cards, channeling messages from the Universe, or doing any other spiritual activities you feel called to do, you'll receive visions from your Soul. These visions will give you a blueprint of why you're here on Earth, what your unique gift is, and how you can create a life you love. Once you receive those visions, you must act on them to manifest your heart's dream life.

Taking disciplined daily actions, eating nutritious food, and finding playful ways to express your creativity are all possible actions you can take to root your energy down to Earth and realize those higher visions in material form. The higher and lower chakra activities I share are examples that may not apply to you. Only you know what your heart is guiding you to do, but it's essential to give yourself permission to express all parts of yourself, including the ones you have shame around.

An essential part of self-love is being honest about all your heart's desires, whether they're spiritual, intellectual, sexual, or material. All your heart's desires exist for a reason, and once you love every part of yourself without denial, you'll find that abundance flows into your life as effortlessly as crystal-clear water travels down a snowy mountain in spring.

11

YOU DESERVE A BEAUTIFUL LIFE

Choosing to love yourself is the best thing you can do to manifest all the money needed to live your heart's dream life. When you love yourself, you trust what your heart tells you and follow your intuition because you know you deserve to live the beautiful life you're capable of creating.

There is a popular belief in your world that says self-love is a challenging goal that is rarely achieved. The truth is, loving yourself is your most natural state. Your essence is pure love, and the only reason you may not feel this way now is that you've forgotten who you are. You're the Universe's infinite, divine love manifested into a unique and unrepeatable form.

You're a child of an unconditionally loving and

benevolent Universe that only wants to see you thrive. The love the Universe has for you is a stream of never-ending light you're always connected to. There is nothing you can do that would stop the Universe from loving you. Knowing that you're always loved will help you see that you deserve all the blessings the Universe wants to give you.

The Universe wants you to be genuinely happy and overflowing with childlike joy. You don't have to compromise any part of your life and say it's okay because you're blessed in other ways. Acknowledging that you have desires in your heart that aren't fulfilled yet doesn't mean you're being ungrateful for what you already have. It's great to be in love with your present life while also looking forward to manifesting more of your heart's desires in the future.

Part of loving yourself is embracing all your heart's desires without convincing yourself that some of them aren't important or realistic. The Universe isn't thinking to itself that you can only have half of your heart's desires met because satisfying all of them would be too much. To an infinite, unconditionally loving Universe, there is no difference between helping you manifest a loving family and helping you manifest a loving family and be wealthy.

You're a beautiful Soul who deserves to feel safe and experience immense joy simply for being alive here on this beautiful planet. You're always loved unconditionally, and there is nothing you can ever do that would stop the Universe from loving you. It's time to surrender the weight of your past and shed any old beliefs that say you don't deserve to be happy. Your happiness is an inspiring light that brings out the best in all the beautiful Souls you cross paths with.

If you're afraid to fully open your heart and receive all the Universe's abundance, it may be because of a limiting belief you learned in your childhood. As a child, you were born freely expressing your inner light without any self-imposed restrictions. As you were shining your light of love onto the unconscious darkness of others, you may have come to believe that because you exposed darkness in others, you were also its source. This might have led you to hide your inner light from the world because you unconsciously associated your carefree, childlike joy with darkness.

None of the darkness you experienced during your childhood is your fault. It's not your fault that you grew up in a world that has experienced so much pain. Shining the light of your love onto the world's darkness is part of your unique gift. When you fully open your heart, you become a pure channel for the Universe's infinite, unconditional love to pour through. Your entire life's journey until this point has been leading you back to that pure state you existed in as a child, but with the inner knowing and recognition that you are love.

All your heart's desires were placed within you because their fulfillment brings immense joy to you and your world. The collective benefits tremendously when you satisfy all your heart's desires. You're not doing anyone any favors when you decide that you don't deserve a life that is too good. You're worthy of receiving all your heart's desires, and they'll come to you when you realize you deserve a beautiful life.

PART III

HARVEST THE FRUITS

12

HEAL YOUR DIVINE WOUND

THERE IS NO AMOUNT OF MONEY THAT CAN BRING happiness into your life that isn't already there. Before you can become wealthy, you must go within and find what hidden part of yourself believes having more money will save you. Becoming abundant is a beautiful thing that will bring so much joy into your life, but it's not a substitute for doing the inner work necessary to manifest your heart's dream life.

Some people use the pursuit of money as a distraction to avoid facing their inner shadow. If someone has enough money to meet their essential needs but still suffers, they may tell themselves more money will fix all their problems. It's often easier and more comfortable for someone to blame a lack of money for their unhappiness than it is to do the painful inner work necessary to heal the root cause of their suffering.

Money can bring joy into your life by giving you the freedom to express your creativity without limits, but it's not a substitute for doing the inner work your Soul came here on Earth to do. If you want to experience true wealth, you must go within and heal your divine wound.

Your Soul chose a divine wound to experience before incarnating on Earth. Healing this wound is the final step in fully expressing your unique gift. You're born to feel heartfelt joy simply for being alive, and all you must do to become the radiating ball of sunshine you're born to be is heal your divine wound. *Why have you been running from yourself?* The answer to this question is the key to receiving the heartfelt joy you've been waiting your whole life to experience.

If you don't face your inner shadow, genuine happiness may seem to elude you regardless of how wealthy, praised, or loved you become. To experience ecstatic joy, you must unlock your unique gift by facing your inner shadow. Only you know what you've been running from and what you must do to heal your divine wound. *Why have you been avoiding the place deep within your heart that carries all the treasure you seek?*

The Universe loves you infinitely more than your ego can imagine and is always holding you, no matter how dark and scary your inner shadow may appear to be. The darkest thoughts and energies are all made up of love but are often heavily disguised. You live in a benevolent Universe that exists to teach your Soul lessons that can only be learned through courageously facing your inner shadow and healing your divine wound. Money will always be waiting for you on the other side of this inner work, but first, you must have the courage to finish walking your unique path to wealth.

Your Soul has purposefully selected a specific divine wound for you in this lifetime because it's through the journey of discovering what it is and how to heal it that you'll unlock the fullest expression of your unique gift. You must go within and face your inner shadow to find the treasure you seek. Your heart always knows the way, but fear may convince you that you don't know what to do. If your ego is pretending that you don't know how to find and face your inner shadow, it may be because it would rather not face the reality that it knows what to do but it's too scared to do it.

Once you've faced your inner shadow and healed your divine wound, you'll be a fully embodied Soul, shining your light everywhere you go. As a fully embodied Soul, the number of people you'll help simply by existing is significantly greater than your ego can imagine. The presence of a Soul's light is like a sun radiating the warm embrace of love everywhere they go.

When you begin showing up in the world as a fully embodied Soul without hiding behind any masks, some people may be triggered. Seeing someone live as their authentic self can be challenging for those who believe they must hide their true selves and adopt a fake personality to survive. When people are triggered, they may say hurtful things because they're projecting the judgment they have towards their repressed selves onto you.

You must never forget that other people's projections aren't personal. Although people who hide behind a mask may be triggered by an authentic presence, deep down, they admire you because they wish they had the courage to embody their true selves. The best way to respond to other people's negative projections is to witness them with love and compassion while remembering they're the result of an inner battle that most people face at some point in their lives.

Your ego's desire for money can be used as a powerful catalyst for a spiritual awakening. Although it may feel like more money will make you happier, becoming rich by playing the part of someone you're not won't bring you true fulfillment. If the source of your wealth comes from wearing a mask, you'll always feel unsatisfied because the money you're receiving validates a fake version of yourself while your true self remains hidden. The path to an abundant and joyful life requires you to courageously shine the light of your Soul in the world.

If you want more money to enter your life, focus on facing your inner shadow and healing your divine wound. If you ignore your inner healing work and just focus on manifesting more money, even if it means hiding who you truly are to get it, you'll create a life that leaves you more dissatisfied than before you started. You're a Soul of pure light having a temporary human experience. To manifest your heart's unique version of heaven on earth, you must take off all masks and live as your authentic self.

The world you're living in now is a playground, and by awakening to your true self, you'll feel the ecstasy of the Universe's infinite love coursing through your body in each moment you're alive. There are no limits to what your Soul can create once you awaken to who you truly are. From this place, you'll easily manifest all the money needed to fulfill your heart's desires.

Becoming wealthy isn't about obtaining a specific amount of money in your bank account. True abundance is about having enough money to fulfill your heart's desires. Some people need millions of dollars to feel wealthy because their Soul needs that money to realize their vision. For others, they don't need any money. Appearances mean nothing; instead of trying to obtain specific material objects, focus on creating your heart's dream life.

There is no joy in owning a large home in the suburbs if what your heart desires is a simple life in the woods. There is also no joy in living a simple life in the woods if your heart desires a large home in the suburbs. Appearances are unique to each individual and are illusions that don't tell you anything about the person they reflect. You're the only one who can listen to your heart and determine what amount of money you need to live your heart's dream life.

To be a genuinely happy, wealthy person, you

must look internally for validation instead of externally. It doesn't matter if your presence triggers others if you know who you are at the Soul level. By waking up to your true self, you're no longer reactive to the projections of others. By seeing yourself as a radiant Soul, nobody can throw you off-center, and you gain true freedom.

The reason you want to become wealthy is that deep down, you want to express the light of your Soul. There is nothing that comes even remotely close to being as satisfying as simply existing in the world as a fully embodied Soul without wearing a single mask. Those who wake up to who they truly are beyond their ego dramatically transform their life and the world around them for the better. When you embody your true self, your presence becomes a catalyst for awakening in others, and you become magnetic to all your heart's desires.

13

FULLY EXPRESS YOUR UNIQUE GIFT

YOUR PLANET IS IN THE MIDDLE OF A PROFOUND spiritual awakening. For the first time in human history, many Souls are simultaneously waking up to their true selves. Without consciously realizing it, your desire for wealth has led you down a beautiful spiritual path. Not only are you on the path to an abundant life, but you're also recognizing yourself as an eternal Soul born to play and create on Earth.

Once you see through the collective belief that the desire for money isn't spiritual, you'll realize it can be a powerful catalyst for your awakening. The greater your awareness of who you truly are, the easier it'll be to attract the wealth needed to live your heart's dream life. Use your ego's desire to become wealthy as fuel for your spiritual awakening. Your

Soul is intimately connected to the Universe's infinite intelligence and knows the best way for you to manifest a life of abundance.

If you decide to ignore your intuition and pursue becoming rich through your ego alone, you'll most likely copy what other rich people have done, creating tension between your Soul and ego. Your ego is a beautiful tool that allows you to exist and play in your world, but it's not your essence. Who you truly are is a Soul of infinite love who has chosen to have a temporary human experience.

Your Soul is infinitely wiser than your ego, but they both need each other here on Earth. Instead of trying to get rid of your ego, realize that your Soul's highest potential is to form a partnership. Choose to see your ego as a powerful tool for your Soul instead of an enemy constantly getting in the way of your happiness. Your Soul has the vision of the life it wants to manifest, and your ego helps manifest that vision on Earth.

A great way to look at this relationship is to imagine that your life is a blank canvas, your ego is a paintbrush, and your Soul is the painter. Without a paintbrush, it's impossible for a painter to paint, but it's only a tool. Your ego is a tool that your Soul uses to create a beautiful life. Your ego will love this partnership because it's through this dynamic that it'll experience a joyful life.

Your Soul came to Earth on an important mission, and part of that mission includes manifesting all the abundance needed to live your heart's dream life. Everything you've experienced in your life up until now has been preparing you to share your unique gift with the world. Your Soul has chosen to incarnate on Earth to help lift the collective frequency of your planet. Everything your heart desires is part of a greater plan to help your planet evolve into the next stage of consciousness.

All your heart's desires exist for a reason, even if they don't appear to benefit anyone but yourself. You're an energetic being who lives in a world of frequency and vibration. It doesn't matter what you do; what matters is the energy you're emanating. Each time you're genuinely happy, you broadcast an energy into your world that makes a positive impact on people you never meet.

If your heart's dream life is to become a hermit in a secluded part of the world, living off a self-sustaining farm, fulfilling that dream influences the collective in a beautiful way. The desires you were taught to deny or repress growing up are likely the ones the world most needs you to pursue. Your heart's desire to manifest more money benefits everyone, even if you only use that money to nurture yourself. The only thing that matters is that you follow your heart, regardless of where it leads you.

Self-love is the key to creating a wealthy life. When you genuinely love yourself, you can never hurt anyone because what your intuition guides you to do is always the best thing you can do for yourself and others. By fully expressing your unique gift, the seed you were born with turns into a bountiful harvest. Nobody else can share the unique medicine you came here on Earth to share. Your only responsibility is to show up and allow the light of your Soul to be fully seen by the world.

ABOUT THE AUTHOR

Eric's journey started with an obsession with online business as a kid that eventually led him to live around the world while connecting with other similar-minded entrepreneurs who love to travel. After living in 8 countries, he had a sudden spiritual awakening during the middle of the night when he began channeling words such as, "Wake up, it's all energy."

This spiritual awakening led Eric down a path of synchronicities, where he completely gave up the business path and went all-in on his spiritual practices. After attending a never-ending list of spiritual classes, from clairvoyant training to breathwork and crystal reiki meditation, Eric found his calling in the dance of life as an Author.

Now, Eric spends his time writing books that help empower you to create your heart's dream life and has gained a large following on the social media apps TikTok & Instagram, where he shares excerpts from his books.

STAY CONNECTED WITH THE AUTHOR

Visit the link below to find all of Eric's books & social media accounts:

www.ericjohncampbell.com

* * *